Such is Life

by
Chaim Berkowitz

Sorry trees, I had to waist a page for spacing.

GOOD OLE CONTENTS

Special Thanks

Preface

WEEK 1

WEEK 2

WEEK 3

WEEK 4

WEEK 5

WEEK 6

WEEK 7

WEEK 8

The Legend of Ted Stevens

Special Thanks

I want to give a special thank you to all the people who serve as a constant inspiration to me every day and who always support me in all that I do no matter how crazy or wild some ideas may be.

I want to also thank those who took the time every day since I started this project about two months ago to read every poem as it was written and give feedback. So thank you so much to my Mom, Dad, Yaf, Ren, Chucky, Rich, KazzieShack, Malechi, Rebecca (FC), Bobby, and of course...E!

In addition, I'd like to dedicate this book in honor of the passing of my grandma,

Rose Berkowitz.

She was one of my favorite people in the world and helped raise me. She was one of the strongest women I have ever met and was a very real person, even in her last seconds with us. She always knew the right thing to say to keep me motivated in life, even if it was literally telling me "when are you going to make something nice for once?"

Everything in this book was written with purpose...Enjoy!

Preface

In a basement in Queens, NY, an artist begins to put his thoughts on paper, struggling to exist within the realities of the urban jungle. In this very room where musicians, wrestlers, politicians, and people from every possible background congregate, one feels and hears the heartbeat of life's story and of the challenges and achievements that can so often lift our spirits and awaken our souls. It is this unfettered diversity of individuals and the challenges of life in today's world that transformed into a collection of poems, each with their own meaning and feeling. The very act of writing down the inspirations and struggles in a world so complex and unfathomable may seem daunting, but when a person dares to express them, he can relate to the lives of so many that find themselves in an ever changing world. This is what this book is about- the fears, dreams and fantasies that surround us. It is a book for those who sit in the basements of our great city and who fight and yearn to revolutionize tomorrow. Each and every entry in this book is a candid reaction to what goes on around us as individuals. The colorful streets of America tell many stories. These are here for the reader to relate to and think about.

The reader will notice upon reading this book that the poems change dramatically in style and context from first to last. This is because each poem was written candidly and the author himself improved and progressed as an individual poet throughout the course of the book's creation. This collection of poems embodies the personal growth and change we go through in our personal lives. The poems are not simply ideas but a blueprint of the authors changing realities and emotions. What could be a better symbolism for a book about life's many realities than one that is itself a measure of its authors changing life? Read these poems and imagine the conditions that brought about each one; you may find yourself in them all.

- Sir Richard Thunderfoot

WEEK 1

Life at 25...

Life at 25...
Well, I'm not doing too badly I'm still alive.

Am I where I thought I'd be...at 25?
Where did I think I would be?
Depends on the age I'd say.

At 5 I thought I'd be a cowboy,
saving the maidens and taming the west.

At 10 I aspired to be an actor,
possibly have my own clothing company.

At 16 I got lost and caught in a dismal cloud of confusion.
There was no future or past, only present.

At 20 I abandoned all dreams and
started studying to be a doctor.

At 22 I abandoned all reality and
kept on dreaming.

At 24 the dream world I created
started manifesting into reality.

So where am I now at 25?

Hey, at least I'm still alive...at 25.

Do you remember me?

Do you remember me?

Do we still live in our tree?

Do we still have our book of past stories and what
we aspire to one day be?

Perhaps because of deforestation the tree ceases to be?

Wait...was there ever a tree? Or just a delusion of what
one of us wanted to be?

I guess you were right, it just wasn't ever meant to be...

In another world

In another world, when pigs fly.
We'd be together, you and I.
We'd hold hands, and sing on high.
Tilt our heads back, voices to the sky.

There would be only love, no room for anger.
I would hold you close protect you from danger.
Nothing could harm you, not even a fly.
No evil would grace you with me by your side.

I'd build us a place to call our own.
A place to lay our heads when weary and worn.
The sounds of little feet would fill the halls.
Crayons and paint all over the walls.

Through life we'd travel the world together.
No bad experiences not even the weather.
We'd find a small village and stay in a hut.
Just live in the moment join in the Wiki Strut.

We'd leave this world the same moment in time.
Our arms intertwined, your hands in mine.
Even in death I'd hold you tight.
Protecting you always, no other ways right.

This world I speak of can be seen at night.
When eyes are closed, soul drifting towards the light.
We'd be together you and I.
In another world, when pigs fly...

The Mystical Fairies of Mount Sprite

The mystical Fairies of Mount Sprite.
No one could see them until the veil of night.
They'd swirl through the skies like flies of fire.
Igniting the world of all its desires.

The curious Fairies of Mount Sprite.
Severely warned by the elders to only fly by night.
Daylight was spent in the old willow tree.
Hidden from all danger no safer place to be.

The ignorant Fairies of Mount Sprite.
Young Lance left the tree in daylight.
Wanted to see the world with no veil of night.
All was beautiful until that one faithful night.

The doomed Fairies of Mount Sprite.
A Snapping Drake picked up the scent during Lance's flight.
Now hungrily awaiting by the tree the veil of night.
The fairies prepare for flight as day turns to night.

The soon extinct Fairies of Mount Sprite.
One by one exiting the tree unaware of such plight.
The Drake sprang to action consuming each fairy in sight
The remaining fairies were crushed with the tree by the left followed
by the right.

The once mystical Fairies of Mount Sprite.
Used to light up the sky in the veil of night.
Now every summer were graced with a reminder.
In the form of swirling flies of fire.

Setting the mind free

Hello me, how art thee.
The time has come to set my mind free.
Who cares about who I want to be?
It's of less importance to me than salt in sea.

Who am I and where am I going?
This is something I care about knowing.
What is my past and what am I doing.
I'm advancing, developing, and finally moving.

There's too much pressure on what people aspire to be.
This is no way to set a mind free.
Just live in the moment the here and the now.
Don't let people's bullshit ever bring you down.

Just find a purpose and work hard at it.
Never listen to other people's shit.
They'll try to deter you and put you down.
Saying "You'll never get this off the ground".

But it's not you who will fail at life.
You get the point while others are blind.
They only care of money and status in life.
World open your eyes and see what you'll find.

A material world is what you will see.
A farce of a world it seems to be.
Where liars are glorified and paper is king.
Our founding fathers never envisioned such a thing.

This world is a world where dreamers thrive.
Any dream in the world can come alive.
Just stick to your guns and never back down.
And you will always get "This" off the ground.

A Legend is born

He stands tall, taller than the rest.
He keeps two guns, holstered to each side of his chest.
Around his waist hang two more, bullets around back strapped in leather.
A sword on his back, tied and tethered.

The man wonders alone, just him and his horse.
Not a soul alive, well not to his knowledge of course.
It wasn't always this way, he used to have a life.
Until it was all ripped away, dog, son, and wife.

Strange days...

A winter's dew, a summer's frost.
Strange days ahead and hope seems lost.
Not all is gone, some still remains.
All our loss is someone's gain.

Up is wrong and black is right.
Strange days indeed, the world fills with fright.
Most hope is lost, small amounts remain.
All our loss is his gain.

We the people have all the power; this will be His final hour.
We've had enough, we decide to fight.
He feeds us lies, proclaims He's right.
After tonight there will be no pain, all His loss is our gain.

Once upon a mid-office daydream

A random thought for this beautiful day.
A plethora of thoughts I'd actually say.
Some random ones about the here and the now.
Some of the benefits gained from the sweat of my brow.

Maybe I'll sail to a mystical island.
Break bread with the people drink something called Widelin.
Perhaps eat the heart of a barracuda.
Lie out all day and smoke some Buddha.

I'd save the village when attacked by monsters.
Remove their masks, reveal they're impostors.
I'd be proclaimed the village king.
Tossed in the royal chair givens tons to drink.

When I pass out they'll carry me off.
They'll tie and bound me to the pole they love.
They'll sacrifice me to their true king
Leaving me never to be heard from again.

True strength

While all the world is sound asleep.
An older man wiggles, winces, and weeps.
He's curled in a ball he wishes he were dead.
All memories of his past sit heavy on his head.

Bound to a chair, what life is this?
A period in time that surely won't be missed.
Perhaps an act of G-d, truly a test.
One can speculate, only he knows best.

Never give up is the motto he wears.
Only he can heal himself if he dares.
One day he will stand, rise above the rest.
He will do all the things, he used to do best.

Ted Stevens

Alone in his room, with nothing but despair.
He swirls, twirls, and fiddles with his hair.
Dreaming of years ago, a better time.
When all was beautiful, his life was fine.

No morning acid rain, melting all in sight.
No bright orange sky, keeping him up at night.
A simpler time indeed, things actually made sense.
When his biggest fear, was paying his rent.

He closes his eyes, leans his head against the wall.
He's instantly back home, family and all.
He sees his son, playing cowboy in the yard.
Wife smiling by the stove, heating some lard.

He can almost smell the pancakes frying.
He knows this memory, sons about to start crying.
A single tear leaves his eye.
Why was he not chosen to die?

His eyes rip open in a fury.
Not a care in the world, but all reason to worry.
The man is tired of being alone.
It's time to head west, dive into the unknown.

He packs his bags and loads his horse.
The rain has stopped; it's time to set a course.
His mind is set to go and find life.
Maybe selfishly to replace his dog, son, and wife.

Wook Jargon

The white horse rode in this afternoon.
For weeks it's been promised it'll be here soon.
What's so great about this horse?
It's set so many before completely off course.

I think I'd rather just go skiing.
See the world from up high; join the famous and the thinning.
Perhaps take a trip, get lost on L Street.
On such a journey there's no telling whom I'll meet.

Maybe just chill with old friends Jary and Mane.
Instead of feeling like I just got hit by a train.
Who actually needs to go skiing or ride a horse?
When you can just chill with Jary, and Mane of course.

On the real

A man enters a store, bomb strapped to his leg.
What can honestly be going through his head?
Maybe about the family he wishes he had.
But the look on his face, it's not even sad.

Perhaps he's nervous about committing a sin.
Actually, no way, just look at his grin.
His actions are about to be glorified in his country.
If he just flips the switch, for a week his family won't be hungry.

How did we get to this point in time?
Why does no one seem to care or mind?
The media is pumping too many distractions.
Numbing people to these evil actions.

The man now nervous, about to pull the trigger.
A soldier shoots him first, but no one could figure.
The man's laying on the floor bloody, now dead.
His pants are removed revealing a bomb strapped to his leg.

Attention: Woman...

Why do women want to be like men?
Don't get the question? I'll rephrase it then.
Why does a woman want to lower herself?
A man in some ways is equal to filth.

Men are like dogs, we are lowly creatures.
Some actually have some canine features.
A woman is a beautiful creature indeed.
Angelic features are what I see.

Women tend to think that men are on high.
But look past the bullshit this is a blatant lie.
Women have been made out to seem second-class.
They have been beaten, abused, and harassed.

The truth is that nowadays,
It's the woman herself that needs to change her ways.
Stop pushing and fighting to be like men,
And a woman will be treated like a lady again.

WEEK 2

Don't take serious!

What do you think the present world would say,
if one day the whole world were gay?
Mojitos would be served everyday at five.
The whole world would come alive.

There would be weekly viewings of Rocky Horror.
We would dance all night get drunker by the hour.
There would be no more wars, hunger, or strife.
Everyone would be happy for the rest of their life.

This peaceful world would be short lived.
Everyone too busy to remember the kids.
All the love in the world and collective elation.
Would only last about one generation.

Watch out Jerry

Green skies and purple clouds.
Pink cats scurrying around.
An orange moon lights the sky.
Not a sound in the air, but it's whistling cry.

The yellow mouselette sticks and moves.
If it stands still, its life it will lose.
The Great Red Hawk circles above.
He has eyed the meal he really loves.

The hawk swoops in, the mouse tries to duck.
Half way in, the hawk is hit by a truck.
The yellow mouselette turns and let's a gasp of relief.
Only to be faced by a pair of pink feet.

Woe to the Cowboy

He quickly took refuge as the purple nova rose.
He dove with horse Lance, under a bridge, rain just missing his toes.
Sat back against the wall and watched the world melt.
A deep hole of sadness is all that he felt.

He tilted his head back, a memory trickled in.
This time a bad one, the one night that he sinned.
He told his wife he would be home late.
Little did she know, he was having a date.

A co- worker of his, her name was Jan.
Her husband died in a crash, she just missed her man.
He had taken advantage of this poor mom.
His wife can never know what he's done.

He opens his eyes, which are cold and wet.
Staring at the floor, he is starting to sweat.
Why did he do such a thing to his wife?
He can't ever say sorry for the rest of his life.

This man is the one who deserved to die
People like this should definitely fry!
The rain has stopped; it's time to get moving.
G-d he wishes he knew what he's doing.

Electric Underground

Electric lights through the midnight sky.
I feel so lucky to be alive.
The bass is pumping, the heart is grooving.
Damn my feet just feel like moving.

Slow it down, now build it up.
My eardrums vibrating, this song is nuts.
Feel the emotion start in my thighs.
It's taking over, I'm so alive!

The harp comes in, an electric classic.
Here comes that ride, my brains ecstatic.
The music flows pure ecstasy.
Whoa! Who's this girl now touching me?

The beat subsides, a melodic groove.
The rhythm is still there, so I just slow move.
Eyes closed, in a trance floating above the world.
Nothing can now touch me, not even that girl.

Summer's night redemption

A summer's day, an eve's breeze.
A wind dances and whispers through the trees.
The sun is setting, day turns to night.
The weather is perfect, everything's right.

Lets hop in our cars and drive down to the lake.
You promised you'd come tonight, you better not flake.
Well run down the dock while taking off our cloths.
Jump in the water, first feel it through our toes.

The sky will be clear, a magical night.
All the stars in the sky shining so bright.
We'll drift on our backs, just floating in time.
No reasons to worry, care, or mind.

We'll sit on the dock, feet still in the water.
Just nature around us, what a beautiful odor.
Fireflies swirl around flashing their lights.
Making this one perfect summer's night.

Basic Training

One eye closes, the other's getting weak.
When will I get the rest I desperately seek?
Hours are passing, it's getting late.
If I could just steal an hour of sleep, that be great...

I'm slowly drifting into subconscious.
Still haven't eaten, my body is nauseous.
Now finally, I'm sound asleep.
This is a feeling I lovingly greet.

Horns blaring, the Sergeant is yelling.
Supposedly outside there is violent rebelling.
We grab our guns, all run down the hall.
Turns out it's just another drill after all.

Mind the Matriarch

A woman dressed in all black clothes.
Exits her home and drifts down the road.
She floats down the path with a look of despair.
The desert wind blowing through her hair.

On the horizon a convoy is proceeding.
The squad should really all be retreating.
Unaware of the danger that lies ahead.
If they continue this path, eventually all will be dead.

But what's this in the middle of the road?
The woman in black, veil makes her unknown.
She warns the men about the impending danger.
Something familiar about her, she is no stranger.

In the blink of an eye the woman is gone.
All that is left is the feeling of wrong.
The men turn around, spooked from the event.
They head home confused, nothing makes sense.

Who was this woman dressed in black?
Why did she warn them of the impending attack?
What can be said with this last breath?
A mother always protects her children, even in death.

Quite before the storm

Wandering through what seemed like a desert, still no one in sight.
Lance keeps trotting along, as day turns to night.
Something is sparkling in the distance.
Possibly water?! Nope, just an old sign from the original "La Resistance".

Food running low, what's Ted to do?
Maybe he can roast some of the glowing tree goo.
He un-mounts Lance and sets up camp.
Hangs up his cloths, which are sweaty and damp.

He lights a fire with hay and rocks.
He takes off his shoes, tries to dry his socks.
He lies down with his guns, makes for himself a bed.
Whatever wakes him up, will be shot in the head.

Carpe Diem

If G-d came to you and said,
after tonight you will be dead.
What do you think you would do?
Would you do something old, would you try something new?

A cliché question some might say.
But how would you spend your very last day?
Would you know how to live another way?
Maybe just run around, zero rules you'll obey.

Perhaps actually spend the day doing good.
Make mama proud like she knew you would.
Just helping people, playing the caring role.
Spiritually uplifting and cleansing your soul.

The whole world will be open to you,
do anything you wanna do.
We should all live our lives like today is our last.
Since the truth is that life goes by way to fast.

Arbitrary Retorts

What if my body gave in to the pain?
What if my soul left me today?
Would I really end up in a better place?
Is the best choice to end the race?

What have I done up to this point in time?
What good have I done so my soul will be fine?
Have I done anything really of worth?
Does my soul really deserve to be on earth?

All good questions these are indeed.
Into the questions one really can read.
I advise however not to waist any time.
Since not a soul can answer any of these questions of mine.

Eyes to the sky

Even though I tend to fall off track.
I know you always have my back.
I don't believe you're this being of anger.
You'll never cast me away and make me a stranger.

In your presence, I always want to be.
Only you can set me free.
You keep me safe from all danger.
While in this corrupt land of strangers.

Everyday I feel your love.
I embrace your light from the heavens above.
As I embark on a venture into the unknown.
I know that I'll never walk alone.

My dear chucks...

I don't think you'll ever know how I feel about you.
I'm not even sure if these feelings are true.
Since the very first time I saw you,
I felt something there, something different, something new.

I don't really know what these feelings mean.
The idea of "us" is probably just a dream.
We met while both going through tough times.
I leaned on your shoulder, you leaned on mine.

Time will tell if you're right for me.
Best friends are something well always be.
An angel you are, sent from above.
Somebody that I will always love.

Dog eat Dog

Two dogs approach the same bone.
One is older, while the other is young.
The older dog looks healthy and strong.
The younger dog looks tired and worn.

The younger tries to plead for the bone.
He claims a far distance he's traveled, and hungry he's grown.
The elder cares not of the younger's whining,
He too is hungry and ready to start dinning.

The younger now desperate, his stomach in pain.
The look in his eye is growing insane.
The elder goes for the bone, pushing the younger aside.
He senses the danger, but can't swallow his pride.

The younger's eyes start twitching, his mouth now foaming,
body aches, his stomach is groaning.
The elder looks up while chewing the bone.
Showing the younger he claimed it his own.

The younger now fuming with eyes of fire.
The elder not realizing his situation is dire.
In the blink of an eye the younger attacks!
Starts by jumping on the elder's back.

He sinks his teeth deep into the back of his neck.
The elder shocked, didn't know what to expect.
The younger snaps his neck, the elder is gone.
Leaving the younger the bone, to now claim his own.

A man named Skip

There once was a man who lived in the woods.
He stored in his trailer a variety of goods.
During the summer he cared for a camp.
At night he walked up and down with his lamp.

His breath bared the smell of gin and coke.
Lucky Strike was his favorite smoke.
He would sneak off at night with his favorite campers.
Took them to the bar down the road called Wranglers.

Everything was great, a simple life.
A natural life, one free of strife.
Until the day that he was let go.
The camp decided they needed him no mo.

What's a simple man to do?
He already is old, he can't learn something new.
He was sent notice to leave the woods.
They wanted him gone, him and his goods.

The camp felt bad, no longer wanted him gone.
However, they were shocked at what they had stumbled upon.
They came to his trailer to allow him to remain.
But all that was there was his trailer up in flames.

At first glance

Her shirt's ripped, jeans tattered.
Gives off the impression she's been battered.
Maybe she's just been living on the street.
Army boots, she wears on her feet.

A tough girl indeed, well at least dressed as such.
Can't really tell by what she's wearing too much.
After starring for quite a while.
It all makes sense; it's just her style.

Is there anybody out there?

He woke one day to birds chirping.
He couldn't believe he heard birds flirting.
Confusion set in. How could this be?
He tried to spot them, but not a bird in a tree.

Ted scanned the skies for these creatures of flight.
"There's no way there are birds." He's probably right.
So what made this peculiar sound?
He's now ready for anything, hunched to the ground.

He slowly takes a few steps back.
Grabs his guns, now ready to attack.
The sound stops, all is silent.
He's slightly relieved it didn't get violent.

But what was that sound he was hearing?
For a minute it sounded like it was nearing.
He forgets the sound and loads his horse.
The time has come to stay the course.

He mounts Lance, takes a last look around.
Ted scans the area but nothing is found.
Something's up, but it's unknown.
Just that sinking feeling he's no longer alone.

Deer in headlights

The wind pressing against my eyes.
This feeling is making my soul rise.
As I whip down the hill, I pick up speed.
I feel the road vibrating in my feet.

Thank G-d I just got these shoes.
No matter the bumps, my balance I won't loose.
My arms are extended to each side.
Deep breath through the nose, I feel alive.

I close my eyes, just take it in.
Don't care about where I'm going or been.
Open my eyes to a sudden shock.
Headlights in front...I'm shit out of luck.

One and done

A day a week enhanced by light.
A day of peace and love, not fight.
One day that could set us all free.
We're all connected as much as we allow ourselves to be.

The day, which is brought on by fire.
A day of which can be used to inspire.
A day, which could be used to look deep within.
We bring it out as we brought it in.

The seventh day of creation,
was given as a day of rest to our nation.
A day for all to unite as one.
Together we can achieve what needs to be done.

The redemption is almost here.
There's no reason we should fear.
Have deep faith in our father above.
When the final day comes, we'll feel the love.

WEEK 3

The Ghost of Girlfriend Past

How long will these feelings last?
Haunted by the ghost of girlfriend past.
She creeps into my thoughts when I'm alone.
Creeps into my heart from a place that seems unknown.

Memories thought to be lost forever.
Burned in the fire and melted together.
Ash was all that remained.
Leaving behind all the pain.

The ghosts of what used to be,
can not seem to be set free.
Living amongst the walking dead.
Playing over in my head.

When will the time come at last?
When I free the memories of girlfriend past.
Perhaps the memories are meant to remain?
Such thoughts as this are in vain.

Post Holiday Block

My mind runs blank, I can't think.
I try to write, now out of ink.
What just happened to my flow?
How to destroy this block I'd love to know.

Shame, since I was on a great pace.
The truth is it's not a race.
How does one get back on track?
When we fall, how do we bounce back?

This seems to be the answer I seek.
Just keep on writing, until my hand's weak.
When a problem rears its ugly face,
dive deeper in to get back on pace.

Black Magic

If you want to see the world of the forsaken souls.
I'll show you how deep the rabbit hole goes.
A potion could be made, to put in your eyes.
From that moment forward, it will all seem like lies.

First take the placenta of a third generation black cat.
Burn it and put the sifted ashes in a vat.
Add a little water to create a paste.
Now put it in the corners of your eyes, no time to waist.

Before doing this, I must warn you what you'll see.
You'll probably spend your life hiding in a tree.
You will see the world from the evil side.
Evil spirits and demons will no longer hide.

You will start hearing little voices in your ear.
Little voices whispering things instilling fear.
Asking you "How could you?" and why you did the misdeed.
These voices are the souls you wasted when spilling your seed.

Now you must think before you act.
Are you really ready for this spiritual attack?
It's probably best to leave this potion alone.
Something's are better left unknown.

WEEK 4

A Pirates Life for Me

There once was a man who lived at sea.
He thought to himself "What a great pirate I'd be.
I'd sail the ocean in search of gold.
Spend my life hunting treasure until I was old."

He sat back in his Captain's chair.
While weaving his fingers through his hair.
He envisioned a whole life for himself.
One filled with adventure and wealth.

He jumped up and announced to the ship.
"Hear me crew as we embark on a trip!
We will sail to a town whose roads are jewel laden.
I'll take for myself one of their fair maidens."

The man continued to ramble on.
When he turned around, the crew was gone.
A pirate ship was approaching "Oh no!"
The crew was preparing down below.

The man jumped up on the rail.
He announced to the pirate ship "If you attack, you will fail!"
The first canon ball shot, hit him in the chest.
No need to get graphic, one can assume the rest.

In over my head

Standing here surrounded by people, unable to move my feet.
My brain entranced by the melodic tones, inside I feel the beat.
Strobe lights flashing all around.
I can no longer feel the ground.

Two women now dancing on each side of the stage.
I have totally lost track of my age.
I can't help but feel lost as I look around.
Wondering through life in a world of trippers, it's hard to find ground.

The beat now takes on a tropical tone.
The crowd erupts, becoming carnival drones.
Finally I can move my feet.
I'm saved by my heritage, hidden within the beat.

American Conspiracy

Today the world thinks Osama is dead.
Took ten years to cash in on the bounty on his head.
This week Obama finally did one thing he promised to do.
Next week Trump will be asking for the death certificate too.

Osama is said to be buried at sea.
This is surely a conspiracy to be.
Supposedly he was found in his mansion.
Laughing at the world, looking for him in a canyon.

At least for now he's supposedly dead.
Put to sleep by a shot to the head.
The world now in an uncomfortable peace.
Since at this point in time he's worried about the least.

Night of the Pagan Carnival

Once upon a magical trip.
A show that won't be forgotten quick.
One full of love and ecstasy.
One of total debauchery.

Lost in a crowd overwhelmed with emotion.
Beneath my feet it feels like an ocean.
The instant classic wishes me well.
The flower girl screams, "We're all going to Hell!"

Outside, it's the British invasion.
What a random and mindless conversation.
These women were anything but classy.
One claimed her throat was dry as a nun's nasty.

A journey commenced to find some food.
Every person picked up along the way, was in some way lewd.
Finally, ended our journey at Tiberius.
Once there, the Brits decided not to eat with us.

With a full stomach we headed home.
What a night full of the unknown.
A magical night it was indeed.
Now all I want is some F-ing sleep.

Congratulations! It's a DoLo!

This world has made me tired and worn.
Time for my street child to be born.
I'm going out, riding solo.
A new writer is born, his name is DoLo.

Tonight will be his first test.
Well see if he can rise above the rest.
One wall, one hydrant, one sewer drain.
This will only be the beginning of DoLo's fame.

DoLo sits in his office, envisioning tonight.
He hopes to G-d everything will go right.
He's sketching designs; he's making a plan.
With G-d's help, he won't encounter the man.

The lost city of New York

The lost city, once called New York.
Now deep under water, people still go to work.
Everyone forced to buy scuba gear.
Now however, there is a new set of fears.

Instead on simply just watching your back.
You need to look all around, weary of a shark attack.
All the ferries have been turned into subs.
People now have jet skies sitting on dubs.

Businessmen now wear business wet suits.
Someone actually came out with wingtip water shoes.
The homeless evolved and now have gills.
Though rusty, still rappers won't take out their grills.

The mermaid parade glides down fifth.
If they step out of line, they will be dealt with.
One fowl word about the oppressors above.
There will be fresh food when the tide rolls in for the doves.

The Hunt is on

He feels her touch lightly on his face.
Her arms around him, he remembers his wife's warm embrace.
In his dream, he looks into her eyes.
He sees her soul, it's still alive.

Looks down, to see his son pulling on his pants.
He yearns to be held too, Ted's hands are full, he can't.
This is a moment for him and his wife.
A moment he'll take with him the rest of his life.

A twig snaps, eyes now opened, Ted scans the room.
Again, has that sinking feeling of doom.
He notices the door is open a crack.
Now uneasy, the door was locked from the back.

He gets up and closes the door.
Turns around, shocked by what's on the floor.
His sword is missing and written in what seems to be blood.
"We have the woman that you loved."

"How is this possible? There are people alive?
And how would they possibly have my wife?
I buried her myself with my two hands...
I dug the hole using our family pans..."

Ted was now full of raw emotion.
These people will pay for causing this inner commotion.
Whoever did this got the attention they want.
Ted loads all his guns; he's now on the hunt.

Windex

A bird swoops in from up ahead.
Crashes beak first into the windshield, now is dead.
Perhaps an act of suicide?
Perhaps the bird just had bad eyes and died?

Where was this bird going or coming from?
Maybe flying in a race and just won?
What if he just got in a little bird fight?
Do you think his bird wife cares if he's all right?

Does he have any eggs? Maybe a chick?
Any chance to survive, now that their dad picked the short stick?
A lot of questions about this bird.
All of which are quite absurd.

Circle of life

One fine winter's day.
Out popped a rabbit named Ray.
She was a beautiful rabbit, ears to the sky.
All the hairs she passed would gasp "Oh my!"

Spring was here, time to get in shape.
Ray of course, now looking for a date.
Summer, soon, will be here.
She awaits those nights, when love is in the air.

Summer came and went quick.
She met her mate by the old willow stick.
She spent the whole summer with him rolling around.
They were so in love, she felt as if she were floating off the ground.

Fall rolled in with a slight chill.
Ray stuffed her face against her will.
She ate because it's what she needed to do.
It wasn't just for her, now she was eating for two.

Winter now just around the bend.
Ray worried for her child, about the upcoming trend.
Her little heart should fear no strife.
Such, is just the cycle of life.

Ode to Ren

What can be said about my dear sweet Ren?
I have no words to describe her, even with a pen.
However, I will do my best.
Since she is currently putting me to the test.

My girl is always dressing classy.
Well put together, but never flashy.
A woman who enjoys the finer things.
Handbags, shoes, diamonds, and rings.

She takes her running very serious.
If she goes weeks without, she becomes delirious.
Once ripped her pants midway through the race.
Her skirt saved her from being a disgrace.

There once was a time that I wanted her kiss.
But all we did to each other was dis.
At first, it always started as fun.
After a few minutes, I was reaching for my gun.

My dear Ren, what can I say?
It's been a while since we got together to play.
Maybe when you come home, well go on a date.
And I'll keep you up, until it's late.

Welcome to my office

Little flowers on the floor.
You sit idly by the door.
Welcoming whomever enters.
A throne a waits, in the center.

A place where people are consumed with thought.
A place I tend to write a lot.
All is silent, only the fan is heard.
What sits in the throne? I chose not to say the word.

It's shit...

No go for DoLo

Let's check back in with our man DoLo.
Seems like he's still riding solo.
Couldn't find last night a friendly spotter.
A look out man, to keep an eye out for Lieutenant Docker.

Tonight however, is another night.
Maybe tonight, he'll do it right.
One wall, one hydrant, one sewer drain.
Hopefully by tomorrow, people will know his name.

Good Morning America

In a world, where nothing is what it seems.
A world made up of pure energies.
A veil covers this magical world.
The veil of material, gives our mind a twirl.

Instead of taking the time to harness our worlds energy.
We spend our time being what the media wants us to be.
Mindless drones, worried about some random prince.
The idea of such nonsense is making me wince.

Why can't the media do what they should?
Which is to for once, promote something actually good.
Will a time ever come, while I still can breath,
That people will focus on the real world, not the one on TV?

A real world exists, but currently can't be seen.
If you use your brain for a second, you'll know what I mean.
The world which all people are created free.
The one that this world is supposed to be.

We all need to wake up, before it too late.
The media and bullshit are having a date.
Rise up people! Don't give up hope.
Start by just putting down the remote.

Poor Little DoLo

No wall, no hydrant, nor sewer drain.
Looks like our man let us down again.
I don't mean to insult or dis.
But maybe he's just not cut out for this.

Everything went according to plan.
There was no run in with the man.
As soon as he approached the wall,
his knees started shaking, felt like he's going to fall.

Nervous, he quickly wrote his name.
Only got paint on half the roller, what a shame.
Instead of it boldly saying DoLo.
Paint dripping all over, looks more like HoMo.

After the wall, he headed home.
He dumped the paint, just wanted to be left alone.
Tonight he feels he failed his test.
With this mentality, he'll never rise above the rest.

Half empty or Half full?

Why are people depressed when it rains?
What's in the water that brings out the pain?
Nothing kills your mood like a gloomy day.
There's not a person who doesn't wish this wasn't the way.

The rain contains a power in itself.
Channeled the right way, could bring spiritual wealth.
Look past the preconceived notion that rain is bad.
Forget the idea that rain equals sad.

A rainy day is a beautiful thing.
We should all run outside in the rain and sing.
You don't need to ask a famous detective.
To know one of the secrets of the world...It's all about perspective.

Moderation is key

Funny how in moderation most things are good.
Like drugs, coffee, even food.
Once you take that step toward excess.
Your body is about to become a hot mess.

Drugs are fine in small doses.
Take too much; see if you feel like roses.
Coffee is great, though can taste bitter.
More then a few cups, you'll have serious jitters.

You'll get the feeling of a cold sweat.
But touch your skin, it won't be wet.
Then you'll feel that nervous wave.
If you only drank one or two cups, your day would be saved.

No mid-day stomach aches.
No rumbling and tumbling or body quakes.
No need to overdue it on food.
It'll make you feel bloated and ugly, put you in a bad mood.

Be healthy and stay true to yourself.
Don't act as if you're rolling in wealth.
Just live a life of moderation.
It'll keep you from ending up someone's patient.

Little Blue People

Three little woodland elves.
Loved messing around in Gargamel's shelves.
They would mix his potions and rip his books.
Drank some stuff that changed their looks.

What's a little elf to do?
Once his skin is changed to blue.
The elves just had to face the fact.
There is no way to change them back.

How will they ever be allowed back in the clan?
They had to devise a new life plan.
Start a new clan of blue elves!
They made huts in the forest out of pieces of shelves.

The two elves got together to make a bet.
Who would be the first to sleep with the elfete?
She actually wanted them both at the same time.
Neither of the elves seemed to mind.

They needed to populate their new clan.
This seemed to be the only logical plan.
If a problem arises, something needs to be done.
Might as well do it while having fun.

Aqua-Lung

I see you watching me through the glass.
You just sit and watch and let time pass.
I roam around in my little zone.
Outside, a whole world to me unknown.

One day, will there ever be?
A time, when I can roam the world with the free.
There's only one thing that I really wish.
Not to be trapped in the body of this fucking fish.

5 - 0

Little man hiding behind your badge.
Under your pants, I know there's a vag.
You act all tough with your gun and your stick.
You have no real reason to be a dick.

Maybe you were picked on a lot as a kid.
Perhaps it's something an "uncle" did.
You're probably just mad you'll never get that promotion.
I wonder how many people are wishing you'd drown in an ocean.

You have been given a chance to protect the people.
Instead you abuse your power and use it for evil.
You think you're the man, on a pedestal above us all.
Here's a sad truth, not a soul will be at your funeral.

WEEK 5

Easy does it

There is a man who walks alone.
With every step, identity becomes more unknown.
Lost in a city that neglects sleep.
He puts on his boots, since the shit is getting deep.

His pockets are bare, as is his fridge.
He makes his way to the rails of the bridge.
He assesses his life while peering out at the river.
He's getting nervous, feels a strange pain in his liver.

While standing there, contemplating suicide.
A feeling rises in him, some small sense of pride.
This is not a person he ever wanted to be.
He's better than this, most people would agree.

What brought him to this place in his head?
Standing on the rail of a bridge, moments from dead.
Takes a second to look at his life, while staring at the water.
Once gone, what will be of his two year old daughter?

He can't do it, the thought is too much of a bother.
No way he can let his daughter grow up with no father.
He turns around and takes a breath.
Slips on the rail, now accidentally plunging to his death.

Domestic Disturbance

In the corner of her room, she sat and wept.
A notebook of anger and love she kept.
At least she had something to keep her sane.
All the yelling and fighting, was damaging her little brain.

This little girl was only ten years old.
She needed a jacket, her life was so cold.
What did she do to deserve this?
Why did her father kiss with his fist?

She prayed for someone to take her away.
Someone to step in and save her day.
A person who would always treat her well.
Never leave her side, unless he tripped and fell.

When will her Romeo come?
Hopefully, he won't be in the form of a gun.
She deserves the best, she's so sweet.
Her other half, she soon will meet.

For now, she just sits and cries.
There's hardly any water left in her eyes.
She rolls over and tries to sleep.
But the sounds from outside the door are cutting her deep.

Cathouse

Exiting the door he trips over a head.
Scatters to his feet "Shit! It's Lance who's dead!"
The sword was used to free the head from the body.
A note was tied to the sword, on the bottom read, "Find me".

Who was this mystery man?
He started his journey through what seemed like the Sudan.
As he walked, he cleaned and sharpened his sword.
Keeping him from getting restless and bored.

The only thought, flowing through Ted's head.
Was in what way, this phantom will end up dead.
Perhaps he'll leave him as he left Lance.
Maybe just use his guns, blow him out of his pants.

On the horizon he saw a dome.
"This must be the bastards home."
Finally, he approaches the doors.
They creek open to reveal a room of...whores?

LéShonda

Ignorant woman on the phone.
I wish you'd just leave me alone.
You crawled out of your little hole.
To inflict the world with your personality, which is dull.

So quick to judge, when you're just a voyeur.
Questioning me like some hopped up Lawyer.
How dare you harass me!
No one grows up saying you are who they want to be.

You lecture me about responsibility.
Tell me I'm as neglectful as can be.
If you looked at your own life, you'd sit in the corner and sob.
So bitch, stop hassling people and get a real job.

The elusive Copper Headed Cobra

Little voice inside my head.
Telling me I want something red.
I attempted this venture once before.
Approached it wrong and ended up sore.

Now I know how to handle this.
An opportunity I actually want to miss.
Why run through a field of daisies,
With all these fiery little crazies?

Today I know what I want.
To be focused on things of more importance, like fonts.
Tomorrow brings another day.
Time to let red slip away.

DoLo no longer SoLo

Well that was quick, our man's beat.
DoLo no longer interested with the street.
He wants to reach people in another way.
One that won't have him put away.

He now uses a canvas, instead of a wall.
Creates hats and T-shirts for us all.
A new way to get his message out.
A better way to spread the word no doubt.

Now the man has partnered up.
DoLo and Bobby raise their cups.
A company is born, the future's looking fine.
All they needed to do was free their minds.

Corner of 59th and 5th

To the man playing pots across the street.
You really make some sick beats.
Drumming away on your pots and your pans.
You grip tight those wooden spoons in your hands.

Everyday the same monotonous beat.
But every time, I can't stop tapping my feet.
Tearing up that catchy tune.
From the second I hear you; I'm in a great mood.

No matter the weather your always there.
If it's raining, you just put on a hat to cover your hair.
Did you acquire your instruments by sin?
Is there a chance you stole that postal bin?

Maybe tomorrow I'll bring you a conga drum.
Add some flavor; make your music more fun.
Either way, I must say bravo.
You're the most consistent person that I know.

Keep on with your catchy tunes.
Keeping the city in a good mood.
There's nothing really to tell you to do.
Just never stop doing you.

Enter the Heavenly Order

Ted draws his sword and jumps back.
Ready for these females to attack.
One walks out slowly, invites him in for a feast.
Extends her hand "This is a place of peace.

We are the women of the heavenly order.
Sheath your sword and fear us no further.
This is a safe place, where you can be free.
Here is a place you want to be.

Join us traveler, you look hungry and worn.
Spend the night, leave after the morning storm.
We would be honored to have you as our guest.
Come in, do relax and lay in our breast."

Ted did not know what to say.
He thought to himself "Is this really my lucky day?
Traveling months, not a soul in sight.
If I trust these women...will I get lucky tonight?

(Next Page)

(Cont.)

I can't be sucked in by these sexual beings.
There's something here, that I'm just not seeing."
He thought for a moment, staying did cross his mind.
"Sorry ladies, but I'll have to regretfully decline."

"But sir! You just suffered a loss.
We saw you from the roof; bury your horse under the cross.
Stay the night and rest your head.
Inside we already have for you a bed."

Now suspicious Ted thought to himself.
"This situation is as normal as a woodland elf.
How do they really know about my loss?
Is the person I'm looking for maybe their boss?

There's only one-way to see what's right.
I'll have to accept and spend the night."
He sheaths his sword and does as they say.
Walks cautiously up to the woman and says "Okay..."

Personal Space

My good man of some foreign race.
Why do you insist on invading my personal space?
There is no need to instigate a fight.
Just kindly take one step to the right.

Why do you insist on sharing the same handle?
I want to burn that hand with a candle.
You're emitting an odor of chicken feet.
I wish someone would stand, so you can take a seat.

Your breath bares the smell of sewage and cheese.
Is there any way you can breath through your nose? Please!
Finally! The subway station.
Fresh air at least, a refreshing sensation.

Slip on through the subway doors.
Grab the handle; the train starts in full force.
A hand touches mine, someone is about to die.
Turn around to see it's the same fucking guy.

Cold Turkey

Puff, puff on the ole cancer stick.
With every pull, my body feels sick.
Where is the enjoyment in this act?
Smoke long you live short, that's a fact.

But who wants to live forever?
Maybe just find someone who smokes and well die together.
Is this actually worth the pain?
Every pull creating a small block in my brain.

For once I think I should be smart.
Old friend, it looks like it is time for us to part.
Brighter days are up ahead.
Free of things that will cause me to end up dead.

Hell on Earth

On a beautiful Thursday afternoon.
Promise that summer will be here soon.
Sweet smells floating all around.
New life, is breaking ground.

Winter's grasp is finally cut.
Everyone is crawling out of their depressing rut.
A bitter winter it was indeed.
Finally we can sit outside and read.

Spring has sprung, love is in the air.
Every two blocks there's some kind of fair.
The sounds of ice cream fill the streets.
Kids line the block awaiting a truck to greet.

Summers in New York are always brutal.
People forget, in New York you get the whole kit and caboodle.
Fall is beautiful, while winter is death as well.
Spring is very pleasant, but summer we're burning in hell.

Big Deed to Little Deed

Big Deed to my man Little Deed.
This is no bullshit I'm about to feed.
My man I must say I love you.
You and your pretty wife too.

You both are like my family.
I know you both will go through life happily.
I will forever also be by your side.
It took a while for me to swallow my pride.

But now I'm here, older and ready for life.
Soon hopefully I'll have my own wife.
Then well have a family garden party.
All sit outside and drink some tea.

We've shared almost everything in life.
Pretty much everything...except your wife.
I'm sorry I missed your wedding day.
For that there is nothing I can say.

But there is a promise I can make.
Which is never again, our friendship I'll forsake.
I will never miss another moment with you and your wife.
I will keep to this promise for the rest of my life.

Lost Tribes of Israel

How do you unite a people spread apart?
We are all separate but all connected at heart.
Everyone should be living in the land of milk and honey.
But we care way too much about material and money.

We were once twelve tribes of the same race.
Today, were spread all over the place.
Now we just see skin color and fight.
Do you honestly think the first Jews were white?

Tolerance needs to be taught in the schools.
There is no reason to feel segregated in Shuls*.
It's time for us all to come back together.
Time for us all to be again sister and brother.

We can bring the redemption within a day.
Just all love each other, what do you say?
We need to be the light of the world and show what to do.
Because that is the point of being a Jew.

* Shul - A Jewish house of worship. (A.K.A. Synagogue or Temple)

Life Actually

A different world is seen when you die.
One that can't be seen with the naked eye.
Everything looks pretty much the same.
Just no such thing as physical pain.

Everything in that world is done with love.
Such a world is waiting up above.
There is no world waiting below us as well.
Contrary to popular belief we currently are living in hell.

This world is meant to be spent cleansing the soul.
Most people are just digging a deeper hole.
If you continue this way until you're up above.
When your soul gets up there, it might not be greeted with love.

Spiritual damage cuts the soul deep.
If the pain could be felt for one day you would never again sleep.
Be conscious everyday of how you act.
So when your time comes, your soul won't fear being sent back.

Deal with the Devil

A demon appears in my back seat.
Tells me my soul, he want to eat.
I tell him to go and fuck himself.
No matter what he offers, I want my health.

He snidely remarks, "Everyone has their price.
I once bought a soul for a pound of rice."
Taking advantage of desperate men.
Playing the same routine over and over again.

He curls around my chair, now in my face.
His eyes are glowing of all the souls he laid to waste.
Opens his mouth, it smells like death.
I never knew souls caused bad breath.

He first offers me a life of gold.
Nothing but riches, until I'm old.
He is denied, I show restraint.
In return, he offers me paint.

My weak point is hit, but I don't give in.
Maybe if he threw in an extra art bin.
He offers me women and lots of food.
Everything he throws out is something good.

Then he hits the nail on the head.
Something people spend their lives searching for until their dead.
Wisdom he offers, this is something I love.
A match that fits just like a glove.

I trade him the wisdom for my soul.
Now inside I feel a big gaping hole.
What is the wisdom you ask that I gained?
Not much, just that I shouldn't have made such a stupid trade.

Now that's a brew

Ted enters the women's home.
An eerie feeling he should have stayed alone.
"Right this way sir, just follow me.
We have something we want you to see."

They led Ted to a set of double doors.
"Come through here, well help heal your sores."
Scents coming through the door were of something good.
The doors open, it's a long table of food.

Ted stunned by the sight, his eyes opened wide.
Thinks to himself "Is this real or am I being taken for a ride?"
He cautiously approaches the table and sits down.
Lays his sword against his chair on the ground.

"Please sir relax and enjoy the food.
While you eat, please enjoy our dancers, which are nude.
We are honored to have you as our guest.
That is the only reason we treat you the best."

Ted uncertain if this was some kind of test.
He wonders, "Who specifies something is the ONLY reason for getting treated best."
Ted grabs one woman's arm "Let me ask you one thing."
She responds "Relax and drink kind sir, tonight you're our king."

Ted downs the cup, just like that.
"What a strange brew, kind of taste like a rat."
The women all over him now, one whispers "Goodnight..."
Ted's eyes roll back; he's out like a light.

Curse of the Man Code

Last night I was betrayed.
Left behind for some lade.
Great plans set with the first mate.
Last minute cancelled and left for a date.

Now tonight, the couch is my home.
Left here to rot all alone.
What's this? A sudden text.
It's the first mate, his night has been hexed.

A night of drama and on the phone.
He would have been better leaving her alone.
A lesson is learned, he now knows the trick.
If you have plans first with your boys, don't pick a chick over a dick.

Like a circle in a square peg

My dear, I think you've become too attached.
We are not as you'd like to think, so evenly matched.
I know some nights we like to cuddle.
You whisper lines that are very subtle.

But this really is not for me.
At this point in time, I need to be free.
You told me you loved me in that last text.
But honestly for me, it's just about the sex.

Blasphemy

Confusing thoughts of a tortured soul.
What is life's true ultimate goal?
Disappointed by the test of life.
What's the true reason for this pain and strife?

Another question of which he feels strong.
If were here to die, then why is life so long?
Maybe this life is just a sick joke.
He leans back in his chair as he takes a smoke.

Supposedly were here to heal the soul.
The idea of this is getting quite dull.
This whole system is such a shame.
Seems to be just some stupid game.

Later that night he went for a walk.
Stumbled upon a message in chalk.
"Heads up" the sidewalk read.
A plane engine fell from the sky, now he's dead.

Be careful what you wish for is the lesson learned.
It wasn't necessarily this man's turn.
Don't challenge G-d and you'll be okay.
You'll live happily for another day.

Friendly advice

There is something that everyone needs to understand.
Which is I'm my own person, my own man.
Everyone loves to give advice to me.
But I'll never be the person you want me to be.

The things you say might work for you.
But to myself I'll always stay true.
I'm building for myself a life, straight from nothing.
That way no one can say that I owe them something.

Now here's my advice for all of you.
Go out yourselves and start something new.
Actually go and get something done.
Then you can talk about how something is run.

WEEK 6

Down with the Hindenburg

Up in the sky, the DishTv blimp floats around.
The things I would do to shoot that shit down.
Blocking the sun, on a clear spring day.
If I were allowed, I'd blow that thing away.

Your service goes out every time it rains.
The satellite signals are scrambling my brains.
Your costumer service sucks, its subpar.
Your employee's effort doesn't go very far.

However your programming, I cannot blame.
Every service's channels are all the same.
The only good thing about DishTv.
Is that its not Wime Tarner, which should be free.

One hell of a race

"I'll meet you on the other side of Jersey!"
Yelled Sir Robert to Ms. Persey.
She tossed him her white glove.
Something for him to remember their love.

The race was about to begin.
One that he knew he surely would win.
He was about to race in a marathon.
Across Jersey and about twenty-six miles long.

The gun blasted and off they went.
Down the road and around the bend.
Ms. Persey drove quickly to the end of the race.
She couldn't wait to see her loves face.

After three hours she became a wretch.
Just then, she saw him coming down the home stretch.
She started screaming and jumping for joy.
Welcoming home, her lover boy.

He crossed the line and won the race.
Cheers ignited through out the whole place.
Two hours later, they were home setting the alarms.
Right there, he collapsed and died in her arms.

The day time stopped

Out whipped the solar flair.
Within seconds, the world was bare.
A man was spared, it seems he's all alone.
Was just working on a present for his son, in the basement of his home.

A led plated bomb shelter was installed.
It covered every inch of the basement walls.
Everyone outside was vaporized.
Within seconds, their brains melted through their eyes.

The man now standing outside alone.
Crying on the steps of his once lovely home.
A chilling fear settles in.
His struggle for survival is about to begin.

A faint sound could be heard.
He hears it a second time, now a third.
Suddenly dizzy, He feels sore in his gut.
He opens his eyes to a woman screaming "WAKE UP!"

Foresight beats Retrospect

Before you go and try something new.
Keep in mind the future you.
How will this choice affect your future?
Will the outcome be good or some kind of torture?

Imagine speaking with the future you.
Will he be proud of what your about to do?
Always have that person in mind.
Take a minute to think "If I take this will I one day be blind?"

Be careful of who you connect to.
Or future you could end up chopped and screwed.
Always be honest and true to yourself.
Since you're the one who will be causing harm to your health.

Your future is more important than anything.
More precious then any diamond ring.
Think before you act and spare yourself some pain.
That's one step towards happiness, success, and fame.

Hey did anyone see my other leg?

The day started like any other.
Jon grabbed his board and headed for the water.
Walked a few blocks and hit the beach.
Felt the soft warm sand beneath his feet.

He looked out at the ocean and took a deep breath.
Every time he went out, he felt like he was facing death.
A few thoughts would always cross his mind.
The friends lost at sea, he knew no one would find.

Now he was surfing in their name.
In their honor trying to gain fame.
Jon digs his board into the sand, drops down and meditates.
Focuses on how he will ride these giant majestic waves.

After a few minutes he's ready to go.
Takes one more cleansing breath and gets up slow.
Picks his board out of the sand.
Straps to his leg his safety band.

Runs to the water and dives right in.
Lays on his board, begins to paddle and swim.
Gets about a hundred feet out.
Just then, he hears someone shout.

He cannot hear what is being said.
A grim feeling comes over him that he soon might be dead.
In a slight panic that his luck has worn thin.
Turns his head to see heading right at him, a grey dorsal fin.

Smile! You're dead...

Most people view death in a negative light.
The truth is a death is a positive sight.
Even if someone dies in a brutal way,
Still there are quite positive things to say.

In this world we live to die.
Knowing this fact could make some cry.
Instead of being negative, perceive it in a good way.
If you do, you'll be happy until your final day.

We are here to brighten the world and cleanse our soul.
If you do the opposite, it will take its toll.
Live selfish and you'll seem blessed with material wealth.
Chances are you'll also be cursed with horrible health.

When a person is chosen, their time is here.
This is something that no one should fear.
Unless of course, you wasted your life.
Were a self-centered tyrant and mistreated your wife

Then you have everything to fear!
Chances are you'll probably be sent back as a deer.
This will be the only way to make things right.
Since you did everything in a negative light.

The universe will then have some fun.
Making sure you're always on the run.
You will see with your own eyes hunters kill your deer wife.
Then you'll be next, hunted for the rest of your deer life.

MTA ruins the day

Stuck in a tube, deep beneath the ground.
Everyone sits quite, not a soul makes a sound.
People are sliding to the edge of their seats.
Some good words from the conductor, they would happily greet.

What caused all this traffic up ahead?
Maybe someone jumped on the tracks, now possibly dead.
Probably just as simple as people working on the tracks.
Repairing and mending all the cracks.

Why not do these kinds of things over night?
How is halting the commute and ruining everyone's morning right?
Truth is Bloomberg* just doesn't care.
What difference does it make to him if it's not fair?

So now we just sit and wait.
Quietly acknowledging we all will be late.
How much better would these situations be?
If we were all friends and acted like family.

*Bloomberg - Micheal Bloomberg (2011 New York City Mayor)

Mr. Snuggles

Under the moon lit summers sky.
A man lies on the ground and wonders why?

Why was he left all alone?
Why did this happen a block from his home?

Why did this happen right after a date?
Why is he still laying on the floor as the night is getting late?

He tries to move, but his leg is done.
He reaches for his phone to call his son.

The man rolls over, lays his hand on his brow.
Now, has only questions of how.

How did his phone get so far?
How was he not fast enough to get back in his car?

How will he ever walk again?
How will he ever man up to his friends?

This man's situation was certainly quirky.
Since his leg was destroyed by a rabid Yorkie.

Like father like son

The family Diamond was as stubborn as can be.
This man just could not set his mind free.
Everything had to be done his way.
He wouldn't listen to what anyone had to say.

At work he loved to act like the boss.
Because of this, every job he had, he lost.
He married a woman with low self-esteem.
She became codependent, even though he was mean.

Eventually, they had a son named Simon.
Just what the world needed, another Diamond.
The man was extremely proud.
Now he had a successor to teach how to be loud.

Years later, when Simon had grown.
He had himself arrogant feelings of his own.
His father one day tried to shoot him down.
Simon snapped back and buried him into the ground.

His father shocked, finally shut his mouth.
His arrogance shrunk and headed south.
What was learned from his son Simon?
Only a diamond can cut another diamond.

Going Green

The artesian waters from the island of Fiji.
Waters as clean and eco-friendly as can be.
Waters so pure and as clear as crystal.
Take one drink it will make you whistle.

The water seeps through underground, maneuvering through rock.
It frees itself of pollutants, which cause bodily shock.
Not a single drop is touched by man.
Until the bottle itself is in your hand.

They pride themselves on how they are so clean.
But it's all just a lie, which is actually mean.
The water itself might be taken in an eco-friendly way.
However they pump thousands of gallons of jet fuel in the air everyday.

It's so kind of them to make the trip.
But how many species died for that landing strip.
Everyone says these days they are going green.
Try to look behind the smiles, what does that really mean?

You in the back

"WAKE UP!" Someone yelled while throwing water in Ted's face.
Ted cracked his eyes open "I should have known the drink was laced."
He tried to move his arms, but they were tied tight.
"On the bright side, at least I finally slept a night."

"SILENCE!" The possible man billowed at Ted.
"You should be thankful you are not yet dead.
Choose your words wisely but answer me straight.
What business brought you to our gate?"

Ted let out a laughing breath.
He knew these women would not be his death.
"You're really going to take the oblivious stance?
I know it was you who killed my horse Lance!

If not you, then surely you saw who it was.
One of your girls made a comment, so at least she does.
Bring forth the one who I met at the gate.
The one who was sent out as live bate."

"NO ONE HERE SAW A THING!
Only in the morning we noticed you when we approached the roof to sing.
Listen carefully, for I'll give you one last chance.
What brought you to our home and don't dare say Lance!"

Ted now in an awkward place.
The truth was Lance, but the truth they didn't want to face.
He decided to lie and just say he found their home.
"I was just curious when from a far I saw your dome."

"WHAT IS THIS LIE YOU JUST SAID?!
I've had enough of you, OFF WITH HIS HEAD!"
One woman grabbed his sword now ready to hand Ted his fait.
Raised the sword and about to swing, a voice from the back yells "WAIT!"

A doomsday afternoon

In two days the world is supposedly done.
Apparently, the second coming of G-d's "son."
The whole world will begin to shake.
All suffering from one massive quake.

What's the significance of the 21 of May?
For most people it's just a regular day.
While a select few will be preparing for the end.
The rest will be enjoying Saturday with a friend.

How do people come up with this crap?
The only followers they have are a bunch of saps.
They will be in for a real shock.
When Sunday rolls in at 12 o' clock.

How do they go on now with their day?
They thought yesterday they would get blown away.
Some for sure happy they missed such a doozy.
Probably just go about their Sunday and see a movie.

Red Hot American Sewer

What subterranean life is found,
A mile and a half beneath the ground?
Never seeing the light of day.
The farthest they'll come up is the subway.

A civilization not ruled by brain.
Everyone is pleasantly insane.
Living off a steady diet of fried roaches and steamed rat.
Served with a light sewage sauce in a hat.

Once a year they test their faith in the creator.
By fighting a full grown North American Gator.
They feast the night away on lizard meat.
The best part is the tail and feet.

Every now and then I'll flush a glove.
A gift I know is received with love.
How do I know so much about this sub culture?
I used to live down there with my man Fulcher.

Dear Charlotte,

To the Charlotte chilling in the bottom corner of the room.
Know that I constantly save you from certain doom.
Actively combating the hands that wander.
Whose purpose is to send you into a world yonder.

I see you when I relax on my throne.
Stringing together a maze of a home.
Catching any trespassers in sight.
Trapping for yourself all kinds of delights.

For now this relationship works.
You scratch my back and I scratch yours.
However, if you step out of line and exit the room.
Nothing will save you from certain doom.

Footsteps to peace

United we fall divided we stand.
This was never the original plan.
How does this mentality make sense?
Everyone building their own personal fence.

All are becoming more selfish minded.
People everyday becoming even more blinded.
All just worried about independent gain.
Hating the idea that we're all born the same.

World we all need to band together.
If we do then there is nothing we can't weather.
We all need to open our gates and toss the keys.
This is the first step to world peace.

WEEK 7

How bad do you really want it?

Bravo to those who stood up for what's right.
Gave the world a real cause to fight.
Not necessarily in a physical way.
Creating certain vibes, some might say.

Vibes that made some feel a sense of pride.
Great words riling emotion, preparing some for the ride.
A journey of peace was presented once before.
Then, we were too scared to go fully through the door.

Now the chance is approaching once more.
Some have an idea of what's in store.
The world is begging for peace at last.
An issue, which potentially could be fixed fast.

The problem comes from all of us within.
Imagine a world pure and free of sin.
We say we want peace, but is this something we're ready to receive?
Well never have peace, unless we want it as bad as we want to breath.

Nothing's warmer then a cocky sheep.

A sheep once approached a mountain gnome.
Started eating grass right in front of his home.
The gnome angrily looked at him and grumbled.
"You my dear sheep need to be humbled."

"What gives you the right to just eat my grass?!
What information do they teach you in field grazing class?"
The sheep paid no attention and continued to eat.
The gnome now furious, ready to turn the sheep into ground meat.

"How dare you just walk on my lawn!
Your just as bad as those stupid brown fawns!"
The sheep paused and raised its head.
He saw the gnomes face was now bright red.

"Allow me to ask you something my good gnome.
I understand that hut is your home.
But who granted you the rest of the land?
What makes this area yours to command?"

The gnome now tired of this wiseass sheep.
Grabbed him by the neck and brought him to his feet.
Beating up a sheep is not really something to gloat.
But let's just say the gnome is the proud owner of a new winter coat.

Fallen Angel

I just saw one of the most beautiful women ever.
What an amazing story we'd have if were one day together.
Never have I fallen so instantly in love.
Like an angel who blesses this earth from above.

She had the face of a Mediterranean queen.
Her beauty was surreal like in a dream.
The best part is she was naturally flawless.
She wore her clothes as if she was from a country that's lawless.

How did something so perfect make it to Earth?
I would love to talk to her to see what she's worth.
But now I'm stories above the world in the sky.
Just stuck in the office wondering…why?

Why did I instantly get so attached?
What indication was there that we'd even be well matched?
Is she now even thinking of me.
Perhaps what kind of person I could possibly be.

The truth is there is no way she thought twice.
The idea of her caring is certainly nice.
But this is life and not a dream.
Which is probably the only place she'll ever again be seen.

Embrace the Light

The world is introduced to a new light.
One that will illuminate the soul in the darkness of night.
From the depths a spark now exists.
Soon a fire will burn deep in the bodily pits.

Words of passion equal to fire.
Something the soul so deeply desires.
The fire melts anger and destroys pain.
Washes it all away like torrential rain.

Leaving the soul feeling airy and pure.
Clean of any evil lures.
Now the soul can shine bright.
Flooding the world with a pure and peaceful light.

Deep roots

Deep in the forest of Chikoree.
Stood a group of different species of trees.
Some Willow, Evergreen, and an Oak.
Even a few species of the kind you smoke.

The Oak was rooted deep in the ground.
He was confident that he was sturdy and sound.
However, the rest of the trees had most of their roots above the earth.
They wanted to show what their roots were worth.

There was no doubt this was a self-centered act.
Anyone who passed by, they wanted to attract.
The Oak however, just stood to the side.
He felt no reason for a bloated sense of pride.

The Oak rooted himself deep into the ground.
He knew there was nothing that could push him around.
The other trees laughed at the Oak.
They thought his idea of creating deep roots was one big joke.

One day there was a nasty storm.
In the middle of the forest a twister was formed.
It whipped right through tearing up all the trees.
All but the wise Oak of Chikoree.

While all the trees roots only went grass deep.
The Oak had roots that were anything but weak.
The lesson learned from the trees of Chikoree.
Is to connect to your roots and get as deep as can be.

Little Buzzie Aldrine

Soaring through space on his home made jet.
He would be out all night if his parents would let.
Hopping planet to planet all over space.
Taking first in the asteroid race.

Saving the universe one moon at a time.
He takes no payment only cookies are fine.
One day he'll be the best astronaut ever.
He'll do great things and bring countries together.

Young buzz parks his jet by the slide.
Tired of playing and ready to come inside.
Heads to bed since he needs his rest.
Tomorrow he has his final zero gravity test.

Tomorrow he'll embark on his biggest mission.
Everything taken care of even his parent's permission.
All gear is packed he will take the space-bike.
Travel to the planet Esuohgod and find Commander Spike.

Super Nanny

All attention is now drawn to the back.
A woman is standing on one of the racks.
"Do not lay one finger on that man's head!
I know this man! I used to put his son to bed!"

"Come forth my child." Said The Order's Queen.
"Explain to me what you mean."
"I know this man from back home.
One of the nicest men I ever known.

I used to babysit for him and his wife.
One day he actually saved my life.
Now it is my chance to repay my debt.
I'd like to take this opportunity to save his life if you'll let."

The queen decided to respect her request.
She took out the keys hidden within her breast.
"My child, understand we will trust what you said.
But if anything goes wrong it's on your head!"

"Thank you my Queen, I Jackie won't let you down."
She took the keys and knelt to the ground.
As Jackie unlocked Ted's wrists.
She had to know about his son Chris.

(Next Page)

(Cont.)

"Please tell me Chris is still around…
Does he still call himself Koga and wear his ninja crown?"
Ted's face gave it all away.
There was nothing more he needed to say.

Jackie's eyes filled with tears.
"Now I know after all these years…"
The Queen stood up, she's had enough.
Ted could sense it's time to go before things got rough.

"Thank you all for letting me go.
There is something first I want you all to know.
I leave now in peace to find who killed my horse.
I hope for your sake the trail doesn't lead me back to your doors.

You claim you had no part and hide the evidence well.
But if I find out it was you, I'm sending you all to hell."
Ted grabbed his guns and attached his sword.
Said one last thank you to Jackie and headed out the door.

The Tale of two brothers

The Middle East is something people just don't understand.
It's not just about countries like Syria, Israel, and Iran.
It's about where we came from and who we are.
To understand this you don't need to go very far.

Open one of our holiest books.
Go to the beginning and take a look.
You will come across a story of two brothers.
They had the same father but two different mothers.

One son he had with the woman he desired.
The other was born to the maid who was eventually fired.
Before the maid and her son were sent away.
Two blessings were given on that day.

The first he gave to the son of his wife.
Told him he would be prosperous even after his life.
One day his children will be a great nation.
Their success will be a worldwide fascination.

(Next Page)

(Cont.)

They will be blessed with the land of milk and honey.
Be imbued with wisdom more valuable than money.
They will walk the land as G-d's people.
Unless they turn their backs, they will be protected from evil.

Next up was the maid's child.
A person who was born extremely wild.
He was blessed to also be a great nation.
But when the child thought of G-d he got a very different sensation.

A warped version was created that day.
A bizzaro tradition some might say.
Now let's skip to the current place in time.
Look at the characteristics and see what you'll find.

Two groups of people brought together by fait.
Both look at each other and see nothing but hate.
The two nations should realize they both pray to the same lord above.
Instead of hate they should shower each other with brotherly love.

Trojan Shirt

To the insect chewing holes in my clean white Ts.
Could you stop ruining all my shirts? Please!
You already sampled my assortment of colors.
You and cotton are like two lovers.

When will your stomach finally be full?
Move on to something more filling like wool.
You are some kind of addict with a lust for cotton.
If I ever caught you, your day would be rotten.

Maybe I'll just find where you live.
A present is all I want to give.
It would be a piece of cotton with a little bug smaller then you.
Something to eat all of your clothes, maybe even a shoe.

Anti-Self

Woe to the self-hating Jew.
To hate ones own people is an evil thing to do.
What makes you so holier then thou?
You are nothing more than an over fed cow.

Making it seem that your Jewish identity is lost.
Looks like someone missed the lesson learned from the Holocaust.
Your reason for hating is not even true.
Some garbage about the success of the Jew.

Take some time to actually look at yourself.
You yourself are a Jew blessed by wealth.
So what exactly is your issue?
Stop being such an ignorant child, here's a tissue.

Find that inner space

He approached the bench, He was fully strapped.
His mind was focused, His soul was tapped.
Meditating hard about the life he's lived.
How can he better serve his king now that he's not a kid?

Diving deep into the back of his mind.
What is his purpose? Is this his true grind?
Body feels like its slowly lifting off its feet.
Now drifting forward, this feeling is a treat.

He could never meditate this deep before.
He feels the energy dripping in through every pore.
He never wants to open his eyes.
He hopes this is what it feels like when he dies.

Opens his eyes, now he's back in the room.
He wants to go back, he came back too soon.
Tomorrow is another day.
Another morning for him to pray.

The Itsy Bitsy Spider

As a spider was coming down the waterspout.
She fell into a bowl of sauerkraut.
She was coming down just fine.
Until a fly flew by and cut her line.

The spider now drowning, but remembered the old spider adage.
When drowning in sauerkraut just hop on a piece of cabbage.
With all eight legs she pushed ahead.
Right as she reached the cabbage, she looked up to see an incoming
piece of bread.

The bread dipped in and explored the bowl.
The spider got knocked back into the liquid and squirmed out of con-
trol.
The bread was lifted with the spider stuck to the side.
The flies all looked on and swelled with pride.

"That's what you get!" One fly yelled out.
"Revenge is sweet!" They all began to shout.
She should have thought twice before eating a fly.
They all sat back and watched the spider die.

My Name is...

Ted left the dome and looked around.
There was a message carved into the ground.
"How did you enjoy your stay?
Happy to see you lived another day.

Now hurry up and head west.
Catch me if you can, no time to rest."
Who was messing with him and why?
What's the deal with this random guy?

Ted kicks the dirt and starts heading west.
"What is this? Some sort of retarded test?"
A mile down the road he takes a break and sits down.
Just then he hears a galloping sound.

He lifts his hat and scratches his head.
"No way it's Lance, since he's been dead...
So who could be riding down the road?"
He grabs his guns "Things are about to get cold."

The rider nears; it's a woman from the dome.
"Now what? She gonna bring me back to her home?"
The woman gets off her horse "I come in peace."
Ted answers "HA! Where have I heard that before? You ladies second
guessing my release?"

(Next Page)

(Cont.)

"No sir, I left the order for good.
I thought it was something else, I misunderstood.
Then I saw how they treated you.
I instantly knew what I had to do.

I actually know who killed your horse.
I found out from a reliable source.
Please allow me to help you find him.
I know where he's going and where he's been."

Ted took a moment to think
He thought, "I guess I could trust her as long as she doesn't offer me a drink."
He agrees to team up by just giving her a grunt.
Now they both are on the hunt.

"My name is Joan, what about you?"
Ted thinks for a second unsure what to do.
Should he just give an alias like the name of a soda?
He decides to honor his son and in a serious tone states
"My name is Koga..."

Cooking with Bob Ross (Ft. Rachel Shalom)

Grab a half-cup of honey in a bowl.
Add a half-cup of water; now mix it with your soul.
Throw in a teaspoon of salt.
Too much? It's not your fault.

Just a dash of crushed pepper and non-dairy cheese.
Toss in some ginger and make it Japanese.
Take out the chicken from inside the fridge.
Pour into a bowl those chips that on the bag say "Ridge."

Baste the chicken in the pan with that honey mix.
Add into another bowl a bag of potato stix.
Hold up, time for a bathroom break.
I actually haven't gone in hours for goodness sake.

Don't forget to wash your hands.
It doesn't count that you previously also cleaned the pans.
Now crank that oven to 400 Degrees.
Make it real hot like the Caribbean seas.

Ooooooooooh!

Toss the chicken in the oven and boil some rice.
How bout a cup of lemonade? Oooooo that's nice!
Now sit back and take a hit of crack.
Better not say shit or you'll catch a bitch smack.

Now where was I? Oh yea, just take the chicken out after
An hour or so...Rice should be done like 15 minutes after...
I donno, enjoy the chips...I guess.

WEEK 8

Excuse me...Have we met?

A man sat down at the table, his plate was bare.
He leaned back into his newly upholstered chair.
Peered out at the long room.
Figured some friends would join him soon.

Maybe his friends were running late.
Perhaps he himself had the wrong date.
No matter, he sits and waits.
Runs his finger around the plates.

The man has the feeling of déjà vu.
Is it possible that this day isn't new?
He gets up and shuffles down the hall.
He does this while running his fingers against the wall.

The day grows old, a man left confused.
Why did no one come baring any news?
Now uncertain if there ever were plans...
Trying to figure out if these are even his hands.

Best he just lay down to sleep.
The confusion is painful it's making him weep.
Life is not easy for an old timer.
Especially one plagued with Alzheimer's.

Just as promised

In the midst of a random dream.
I heard the voice of an angelic being.
I couldn't see the voices face.
But this was a familiar voice I lovingly embraced.

The voice I heard was filled with love.
It was the voice of my grandmother that recently was sent above.
The voice had the same mannerisms of my grandma Rose.
She told me things that no one else knows.

Said she was welcomed with a tremendous round of applause.
She was shocked to be in a realm, which is free of any flaws.
Unexpected was her soul,
When she passed to the other side and realized her roll.

She warned me of a looming doom.
An event that will take place soon.
The details were about some kind of test.
One I could pass if I could just remember the rest.

Who wants to live alone?

What if I end up going through life alone?
He who doesn't fear this let them cast the first stone.
All you need is one traumatic relationship.
To give your heart and soul a seemingly permanent rip.

What if karma really is quite the bitch?
I'll never be fully happy, even if I'm one day rich.
Life is not so easy without the other half.
Like walking up a mountain without a walking staff.

What's the point of living in a nice home?
When only you can enjoy it since you're all alone.
This is why I need to find my other half.
Someone by my side while walking down this path.

There is no point living a life alone.
Everyone needs someone to share their throne.
Beauty truly is in the eye of the beholder.
This concept makes more sense the more I get older.

Time to stop judging based on the outside.
I need a drink of humble to help swallow my pride.
Finally reopen my heart for what's meant for me.
Embrace my other half so finally I can just...be.

And now! The thrilling conclusion of...
THE LEGEND OF TED STEVENS!

The two ride for hours due west.
Ted riding with authority, Joan gripping his chest.
Night falls and it's too dark to ride.
Ted gets off the horse to set up camp on the side.

"Rest up, tomorrow we ride all day."
Ted stated while walking away.
"Come lay with me please and keep me warm.
Well be protected under my blanket from the morning storm."

Ted gave in to Joan's request.
It's been so long since he's laid against a breast.
"Allow me dear Koga to help you relax."
Joan pulled gently on Koga's slacks.

"It's ok..." Koga muttered while slightly moving away
"Lets just get some rest, tomorrow's a big day."
They both lay there and breathed in deep.
Within minutes they were sound asleep.

Suddenly there was a blood curling scream.
Ted opened his eyes but felt like he was still in a dream.
He was standing with Joan against a tree.
His hand around her throat, keeping her brain oxygen free.

(Next Page)

(Cont.)

Ted let go, shocked at what he's done.
He checks his sides feeling for his guns.
Ted unsure of what to say.
"What just happened? Are you ok?"

"What the hell was that? Are you out of your mind?!
You chocked me so hard I was going blind!
How dare you grab me and throw me against a tree!
Chocking me and screaming about some false treachery."

"I jumped up and started to chock you?
This doesn't sound like something I would do."
Ted confused about what just took place
Suddenly, a blank look on his face.

Of course! It all started to make sense.
 Ted stroked his head and sat back against the fence.
This whole time, could it really be?
"The person I'm looking for is..."

Final Thoughts

Never ever give up! Keep grinding until the day you die.

Don't ever stop loving. Love is the most beautiful and strongest force in the world. Embrace it.

Be the black sheep, as long as you have a positive purpose.

Life is all about perspective.

ALWAYS live consciously.

Never close your heart off to love. Just be careful of who you choose to love.

Always smile, life is way too beautiful and short to waist on negativity. There is always a positive side to any situation.

No matter what happens in life, it is always for the best.

One last HUGE thank you to Yaffa. You are amazing and continue to serve as a constant inspiration to me. Thank you so much for all the help and support you gave during this whole process. I love you very much. Good shit!

16270571R00079

Printed in Great Britain
by Amazon